The Soul in Love

includes
an audio CD
of the poetry,
read by Bill Bauman

These poems are the inspired words
of Bill's soul, shared with you, offering you
quiet moments of peaceful reflection

D1314166

THE SOUL IN LOVE

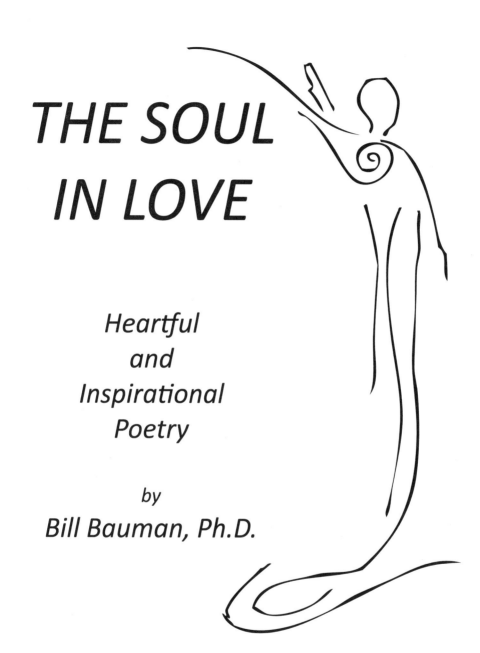

Heartful
and
Inspirational
Poetry

by

Bill Bauman, Ph.D.

THE CENTER FOR SOULFUL LIVING

A CENTER FOR SOULFUL LIVING PUBLICATION

The Center for Soulful Living
P.O. Box 583
St. George, UT 84771-0583
USA

www.aboutcsl.com

FIRST EDITION, 2010

Cover design and interior illustrations by Donna J. Bauman
Book design by Donna J. Bauman

Print layout and graphics treatment by
Light*Works* Media

ISBN 978 - 0 - 615 - 35986 - 1

Printed in the United States of America
This edition is printed with vegetable oil-based ink
on acid-free paper of 12% recycled materials,
meeting the Sustainable Forest Initiative Standard.

Contents

Introduction

I've rarely written poetry throughout my life—except when I won my beautiful wife's unsuspecting heart with an exquisite rendition of the tried-and-true "Roses are red ..." love poem many years ago. In recent years, however, I underwent two emergency surgeries and two near death experiences in quick succession. As I re-emerged into life and aliveness, it became clear that I brought back with me a soul that had fundamentally expanded, was noticeably fuller, and now clamored to speak its love-filled mind.

The poems that follow literally express the thoughts of that newly present soul. They reveal my soul's—perhaps *the* soul's—unique vision of life. They graphically show what the eyes of pure love perceive as they look out onto our human world, and expose how that love-filled perception can change our personal relationship to, well, to everything.

As I witnessed myself writing these poems, it was clear in one sense that I was but the transcriber of a bigger, wiser and more universal source—indeed, the very soul of life itself. Yet, since that soul had now merged with and become my own, I felt my own passion living in the verses as I was writing them, and I experienced my heart breathing itself into the words as they took creative form on the page.

My inspiration in writing this booklet of poetry is to share with you a soul-sourced vision about what human living can be like. So often we are surrounded with societal perceptions and accepted mind-sets that invite us to see most things as problems, then invite us to feel burdened by them. Yet, our souls don't have that heavy vision; they don't know that bleak worldview. Indeed, they see you and me through the eyes of a divinely loving creator—through eyes that know our absolute perfection, our innate beauty, our inherent wonder. These poems embody and express that precious vision.

In the language of several of these poems you'll find the spirit of Dr. Seuss alive and well, giving the message a lightness and creativity that hopefully enhance their message. I wrote the final poem, *There's a Field*, in honor of Rumi, the famous 13th Century Sufi poet who wrote a poem (*Out Beyond Ideas*) with a similar message. I intend that each and every one of these poems speak to your heart as much as to your mind. I envision their words dancing in your mystical awareness, their spirit awakening your free spirit, and their deeper truth enlivening your whole person.

I am privileged to have been graciously supported by my wondrous life partner, Donna Bauman. She has given of her endless artistic gifts to create beautiful illustrations for this book's poetry. Her inspiring drawings surround my words with such grace and give them that extra glow of elegance that they so deserve. Thank you so much, Donna. I love and treasure you so deeply.

Finally, I thank you so much for opening your heart to these poetic expressions of soulful inspiration. May they awaken you to the inner voice of your own soul! May they help you to attune deeply to your heart's own love-filled whisperings! And may you be blessed by their loving spirit every day of your life!

Bill Bauman

Welcome

Hello
I'm your soul
And I'm in love
Yes deliriously passionately and hopelessly
In love

I'm in love with everything that exists you see
But most especially I'm deeply in love with you
And that mysterious world called your life

I have no choice you know
For I'm your soul ... the purely clearly loving you
The you that sees life with unclouded eyes
That embraces everything in its deepest truth
That knows not how to judge or condemn
That cherishes the beauty that resides everywhere

I was with you when you swallowed your first breath of earthly air
and I've lived in your ever-glowing heart every day of your budding life
From this sacred home where I nurture your uncluttered truth
I love you fully cherish you deeply encourage you endlessly
Proclaiming your seamless worth at every turn
Urging you on when times are especially hard
Softly nudging and inviting you always to remember
... to remember

To remember most of all the sacredness of your beautiful self
The perfection of your human condition
The wonder of your majestic life
And the magic of every event that enters that life

To remember the divine touch embedded in everything you see
The infinite miracle veiled within whatever you embrace
And the utter preciousness of every moment of your life
In which you are so tenderly held in this planet's warm embrace

I've written these poems to help you recapture these sacred memories
And to invite you to taste anew my undying devotion
As I whisper the sweet nothings of my wisdom into your inner ear
And fill you with the wondrous love that lives endlessly within me

My wish is that as you experience my poetic words
You will more and more see yourself through my soulful eyes
And experience everything in your personal life as I do ...
As a human expression of divine love and infinite beauty

While you sample these poetic images of my spirit-filled vision
Know that I am tenderly holding you embracing you
Just as an adoring mother graciously cuddles her child
To help you love yourself with abandon
Embrace your worth without question
Drink in life's beauty with awe
And live ... live ... live with soul
Every moment of your amazing life

Creation

There I was
Sitting around just being me
With nothing to do or say and nothing to see
When the simple thought occurred to me
Wouldn't it be nice to have other versions of me
Floating all around this endless infinity

I'm God you know your creative source
And it's not that I was bored or lonely of course
It's just that I wanted to know to see
What would happen if I actually replicated me

So I spoke the mighty word opened the invisible gates
And created life everywhere yes in a gazillion takes
Universes burning bright countless dimensions of light
Worlds without end and of course many life forms to tend
All of them alive dynamic rich all so expressive
None of them imperfect wrong lacking or even excessive

I fell instantly in love with these replications of infinity
So filled are they with my charisma my sensitivity
I found them perfectly wondrous even delightfully thunderous
So I gave them the right to create just like me
And sure enough create they did for all to see
Worlds and scenes big and bold
Fresh versions of themselves first new then old

It was then and there I'm sure you can see
That I saw how limitless creation could be
From imagination to invention from desire to expression
The creations continued in glorious progression
Worlds of options and potential and possibilities vast
Each one more delightful endearing and gorgeous than the last

I'm in love yes in love with creation and its spark
For without it I'd be sitting alone in a space quite stark
I'm proud of myself for speaking the word for opening the gates
And now witnessing creation in this bigger than life space
In their thoughts and deeds in their inventions and events
I can't begin to tell you the ecstasy I sense

I still sit around you know just being me
It's peaceful being alone with nothing to see
But when I want joy or love or sights to behold
I look at my creation and the stories to be told
And I rejoice I salute I leap to my feet
As I celebrate your radiance yes your glow so sweet
I watch you speak your mighty word and open the gate
As you create anew and design your fate

Creation creation we're true peas in a pod

You fulfill and excite me with your slightest nod

Indeed without you it wouldn't be fun being God

What a Sight!

What a sight this swirling twirling earth is
Swishing and swaying through our supple spacious universe
Rhythmically traversing the elastic heavenly bodies
Yet claiming its own special space
Choosing its own robust role
Expressing its own bounteous beauty

What a sight this glorious globe is

This spinning ball of enriching energy of vigorous vitality

As it infuses the wild whacky wonder of life's endless eternity

Into the waiting arms of every creature living on its tender skin

What a sight this plush planet is
As it radiates its love-laden light all around itself
Creating a spacious sphere of unparalleled possibilities
Sharing its luscious life with its deeply cherished children
Nourishing its treasured offspring with its generous gifts

What a sight this opulent orb is
As it reflects life-giving light into the feeling flesh of its progeny
Pulses the life blood of the undulating universe into our heaving human hearts
And loves its holy human issue in a ceaseless caring caress

What a sight this sanctified sphere is
As it spaciously spins its wondrous web through an inspiring spiraling space
Inviting us to breathe its bliss-filled breath and share its shining soul
While supporting us with its empowering embrace and tender touch

What a sight this way out wondrous world is
Filled with life, aglow with love, awash in beauty
How stunningly simple how innately natural it is to love it
Just as an open hearted child responds
To the tantalizing touch of its admiring mother
How endlessly easy to embrace and absorb its generous gifts
How refreshingly rich to feel its soft sensitive sensations
How deliriously delightful to taste its limitless love enlivening our lives

What a sight this resplendent realm is
Our heroic home hovering amidst the glowing glimmering galaxy
Our abundant abode awash in life's voluptuous vastness
Our delight-filled dwelling dedicated to love's lavish light
Our winsome wellspring of infinity's glorious gifts

Thank you ever generous earth
Plentiful planet of loving life
Wondrous world of whimsical wonder
Sacred sphere of boundless blessings
Gentle globe of glorious grace

What a sight this earth is

Sweet Nature

In the tender touch of a falling leaf
And the sweet soft caress of a balmy breeze
Nature kisses us gently generously graciously
Reassuring us of our frequently forgotten worth
Reminding us of our abundant unbroken beauty
Revealing anew to us our much marveled majesty

When nature's beneficent breath surrounds our silent soul
Breathing her life giving love into our humble human hearts
We feel her maternal breast descending sweetly onto our sensitive skin
Her devoted delight playing lyrical love songs in our excited cells
Her passionate piety moving magically through our very veins

As nature's earth air fire water
Ignite their singular passions inside our cells
We are blasted into the eternal bliss
That comes only from the elemental delight
Of their strength, light, passion and love

When nature
From her storehouse of plentiful abundance
Graciously shares her endless love
And precious unseen blessings
We have but one choice—
To be in awe of her beating heart
To feel blessed by her quiet soul
To witness ourselves wrapped in her eternal love

What a bounty has been bestowed upon us
By this embodiment of unconditional love
By this earthly expression of divine grace
By this wonder of creation called nature

What fortunate beings we have become
What countless blessings are forever ours
When we touch nature ... or she touches us
When we witness her beauty ... or she celebrates ours
When we are filled with her gifts ... or she simply stands in her elegance

Thank you sweet nature
Cherished friend treasured mother
Benevolent bearer of ever unrequested gifts
For simply being and for softly speaking
For this moment's gentle touch
For this day's magical embrace
For this instant's eternal kiss

Could It Be

Could it be
That we are all floating and flowing
In an infinite nebula of ceaseless sacred space
Only thinking that we are lodged and grounded in matter

Could it be
That right now we are touching tasting space's luscious love
Are enveloped and enfolded in her indulgent embrace
Are filled to overflowing with her renewing radiance
Are swishing through her radiant rays of luminous light
On an unseen swing of delicious delight

Could it be
That you and I
In this very magical moment
Are breathing life both Inside and outside of time
Are being silently shuttled through and beyond space itself
Within infinity's transforming tunnel of life-giving light

Could it be
That space—
Surreal supportive sensual space—
Is our enriching inspiring infinite mother
The resilient source of our soul's stirring inspirations
The elegant elixir for our heart's highest hopes

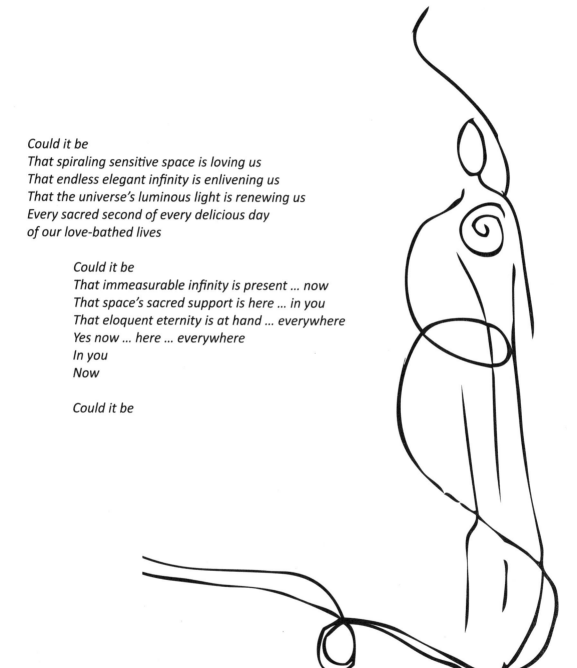

Could it be
That spiraling sensitive space is loving us
That endless elegant infinity is enlivening us
That the universe's luminous light is renewing us
Every sacred second of every delicious day
of our love-bathed lives

Could it be
That immeasurable infinity is present … now
That space's sacred support is here … in you
That eloquent eternity is at hand … everywhere
Yes now … here … everywhere
In you
Now

Could it be

Do you Remember

Look at you
Pure radiant glamorous soul
Beaming ray of infinity's light
I was just thinking about that sacred moment
When your unbounded soul was graciously thrust
From the blissful heart of divine love
Only to land mightily on this precious earth
Generously becoming one of us

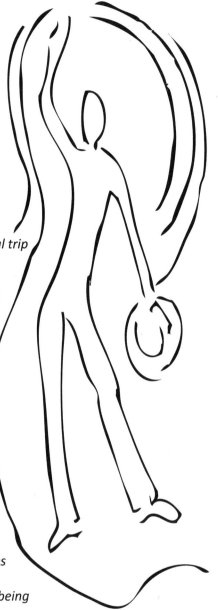

Can you recall what it was like before that eventful trip
Your spirit so eternal so free
Your soul so immense so vast
Can you remember being that brilliant ray of light
Floating gleefully in endless fields of divine grace
Ah you were so amazing so limitless so grand
A ray of bright sunshine to all around you
An unspeakable delight to behold

Now look at you

All dressed up in your very own human body

Filled to overflowing with tender human emotions

Stirred from within by rich dreams and passionate desires

Daily transfixed by heartful creations and chosen successes

Yes you've become an honest to goodness official human being

Good for you
Do you still remember your glowing light
Can you recall
Your beauteous soul your amazing spirit
Your infinite elegance your mystical splendor
Your vast radiance your endless wonder

They're all still here you know—
these dazzling qualities of your radiant past
They're fully alive and well right here and now
In you through you around you as you
Yes, they're as much you now as then

Ah look inside yourself—there they are
Search your beating heart—your mighty spirit is smiling up at you
Find your deepest core—your wise soul is there quietly whispering to you
Dive into your creative thoughts—your endless infinity is shining upon you
Open to your silent depths—your vast light is right there greeting you
Look all around yourself—your radiant glow is shining brightly everywhere

Yes look at you
Humanly divine and divinely human ... matter and spirit dancing together
Earth and universe blended in harmony ... body and soul united in love
Limitless light breathing you and being breathed by you
Unbounded spirit alive in you and swirling all around you
Vast soul inspiring you and blessing everyone around you
Powerful universe expressing within you and expressed as you

Look at you ... look at you

Dance of Life

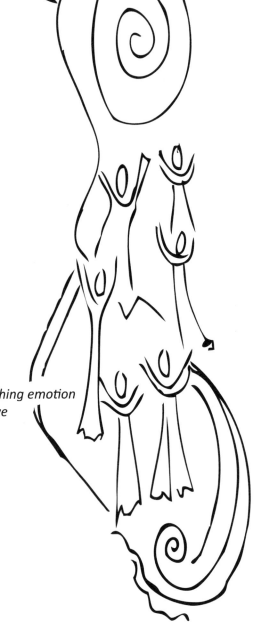

Imagine this
Among the infinite worlds and universes of life
A single solitary planet
Is reserved for dance
For the alive vibrant exciting
Pulsing sparkling dazzling
Refreshing delighting energizing
Dance of life

     Who wouldn't come
     To such an enticing planet
     Once invited as an honored guest
     To this passionate dance of life
     Who wouldn't choose to attend
     This fun gleeful crazy party
     Just when your little inner voice told you
     You could use a little fun

Welcome to the ball
Come in ... enjoy this outrageous planet
In its wild movement and compelling sway
Make yourself at home on the dance floor of touching emotion
Find pleasure in the intimate dance of heartful love
In the sensual tango of energetic passion
In the serene waltz of nature's elegance
In the moving rumba of primal intensity
In the inspiring ballet of life's beauty

How she moves and sways
Glitters and glows
Senses and feels
Breathes and blows
This planet of dancing swirling twirling ecstasy

How exquisite her body
Bending willingly to her sun's mighty touch
How inspiring her soul
Impressing its grace into her very winds
How delightful her spirit
Flowing lovingly through her animated senses

Let's surrender to her party's embrace
Let our hair down, way down
As the spirit of the dance takes us over
Let's find our soul's inviting movement
Open our body's rusty valves
Unleash our psyche's unbridled force
And let loose with our endless might

We've come to the dance
Yes, the dance of life
A dance like no other
Ah the dance of life

Body Elegant

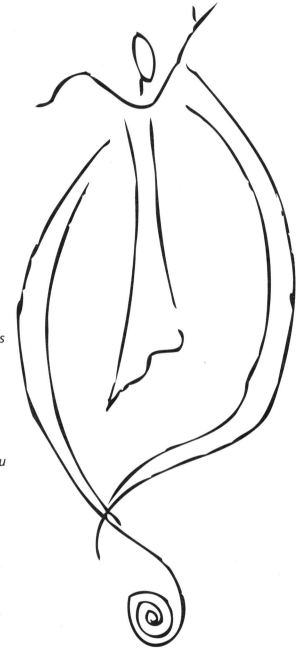

Bodies, bodies, bodies
My body, your body, the body
What sights they are to behold
Beautiful bodies, ugly bodies
Thin bodies, fat bodies
Healthy bodies, sick bodies
Bodies

    My body is gorgeous
    So is yours
    I know
    I've seen them both
    Outside and inside
    They're filled with
    Endless beauty, rich elegance
    Enviable fashion, quiet grace
    And, of course, splendid good looks

Yep, it's true
Your body is the real you
Infinite and divine, just like you
Rich and stylish, same as you
Radiant and shining, it must be you
Sophisticated and chic, sure enough it's you
Your body, the real you
It's how you speak physically
Move sensually
Express gracefully
And breathe chi-fully
Aren't you something special now

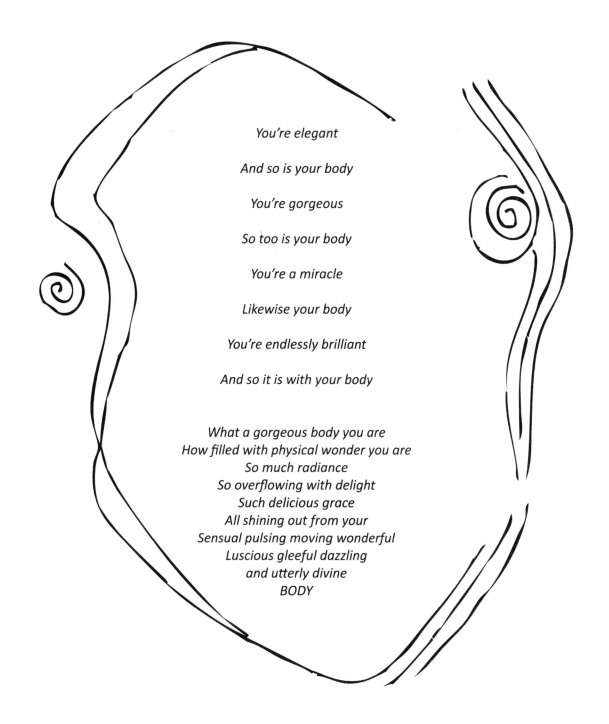

You're elegant

And so is your body

You're gorgeous

So too is your body

You're a miracle

Likewise your body

You're endlessly brilliant

And so it is with your body

What a gorgeous body you are
How filled with physical wonder you are
So much radiance
So overflowing with delight
Such delicious grace
All shining out from your
Sensual pulsing moving wonderful
Luscious gleeful dazzling
and utterly divine
BODY

Just By Being you

Thank you for being you ... for being here
For entering so willingly into our funny silly world
For so smartly becoming one of us peculiar human beings
For bringing your boundless wit to our small brains
Your wild spirit to our dulled senses
Your eccentric light to our darker thoughts

Just by being you ... just by being here
You enhance our tender human sphere
You bless our weary heavy hearts
You honor our busy stressed minds
You brighten our muted but hopeful lives

Yes just by being you ... just by being here

Just because you're in our crazy world

We somehow find our forgotten beauty

We manage to forgive our long-loathed faults

We remember our well hidden worth

We re-open our hearts to love ourselves

Yes because of you

Oh sure we never tell you our feelings of gratitude
Imagine how embarrassed even ashamed we would be
And yes we take you for granted and put you down
After all we don't want your infinitely wondrous nature
To go to that delicious delectable head of yours

So forgive us if just this once
We break our own very important rule
And whisper our long held secret into your deserving ear
Here it is
We really know how much you bless our lives
How generous devoted loving and heroic you are
And, gulp, thank you so much
For being you ... for being here

When you first came to us
You brought your dazzling spirit
your bubbly soul your thrilling light
And placed them gently into our waiting hearts
You awakened us to our own vast spirit
Our loving soul our luminous light

Every day of your life

Your brightness and joy illuminate our lives

Your spirit-filled presence awakens our souls

Your beauty and love tickle our hearts

It's a shame come to think of it

That this is the only time

We'll ever tell you how much we treasure you

Thank you so much
For being you ... for being here

This World of Duality

What a life
Ups and downs ins and outs highs and lows
Topsy turvy brainy and zany fasts and slows
Inside out and outside in upside down and downside up
It's so confusing so baffling so bizarre so nuts

It never stops

This funny world that makes no sense

Runs so wild takes no prisoners is so intense

What a life

So full of risk so hit and miss so rough and tough

It's a world of chance a gamble of luck it's messy stuff

What a life ... we're on the brink... in this shaky wobbly roller rink
Would it ever take a calmer turn do you think
Be more normal be only kind perhaps gentle overall
Would it ever stop hurting stop confusing stop baffling us all
Would it ever give up the ride the drama the pain the strain
Would it ... could it even if it wanted it in its brain

Sure it hurts sure it wounds and sure it's hard
This willy nilly rocking shocking earth of ours
Sure it pulls us pushes us throws us nudges us
But would we want it softer smoother without the fuss
Would we miss the ride the twists and turns that make us cuss

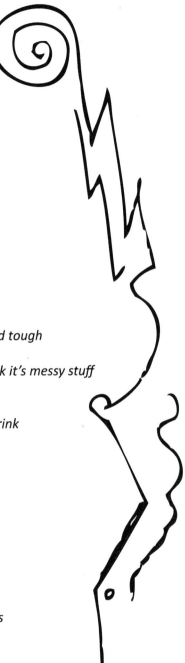

I don't know about you ... but for me
I'd yearn for the jolts the shocks the spurts the dance
The unexpected unforeseen unknown chance
I'd long for the surprising the startling the staggering prance
In this world of opposites of differences of hubbub of rants

I'd pine for the comedy and tragedy the hue and cry
Of a world that knows how to live and die
Of a world that pushes and pulls grows and shrinks
And loves me throws me plays me moves me
On its full spectrum instrument of wobbly instincts

I love this puzzling earth
This realm of dazzling whirling swirling worth
Of joy and misery of laughter and pain of sunshine and rain
This confusing blend of inconsistency and strain
This world of wonder and stress of mystery and pain

Yes I'm in love with its unknowable mysteries its exotic might
That shoots me wondrously to its ecstatic height
Then plunges me inexplicably to its delirious depth
And so gives me the surprise ride of my unsuspecting life
And the surreal real deal feel of the meaning of life

So gratitude is on my lips in my heart in my deepest esteem
As I live love hurt grieve scream and beam
On the wild ride of this planet of whim of this world of dream

Love Song

Imagine love as music
And yourself as its favorite instrument
Picture love as an intimate tune a sweetheart song
Singing its devoted melody of love into your depths
Envision love playing its heart song soul song spirit song
On that perfect instrument of love
Called you

Love sings hums chants plays
On an elegant instrument of sheer delight
That fine-tuned perfectly polished instrument called you
Can you hear love's sensual elegance
Playing its tune and singing its song
In your cells your heart your mind
Through your nerve endings your blood stream
In your feelings your thoughts your whole self

Love is a song that must be sung
Must be heard must be sensed must be felt
It's the irresistible song that sings in our hearts
The compelling song of love of light
The magical song of joy of glee
The endless soaring circling song of life
On an instrument that is one of elegant delight

If I were love playing my music singing my song
If I were love strumming the strings of your willing heart

I would sing my devotion into your veins
Play my zeal into your thoughts

Hum my adoration into your body
Intone my reverence into your emotion
Chant my joy into your feelings

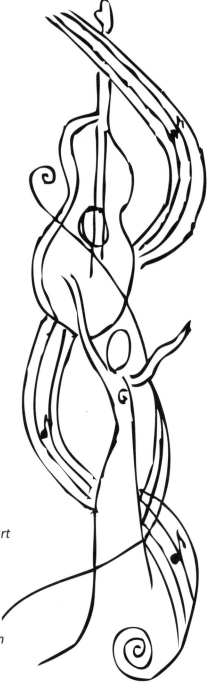

And as I found you listening to my delicate tune
I would croon to you in my soulful melodious tone
About how beautiful you are

How divine you look
How perfect wondrous magnificent and delightful you are

Yes I would love you love you love you without end
In a song of everlasting affection and adoration

You are the cherished instrument of love itself
You are also the irresistible song of life
That intones itself daily from your core
Yes you are love itself
Infinite endless enlivening gracious luscious love
You are the sacred music of life

Sing then your soul's song

Sing it into our waiting hearts

Into our pores through our bodies into our depths

Be the song the song of life

The song of love

Beauty

It was a quiet sunny afternoon in spring
I was floating gleefully gracefully on my vast swing
    In that pure realm of light above our earth that shone so blue
    Enjoying the seamless expanse the endless view
        Of space's infinite spheres and earth's sacred hue
        When an elegant thought drifted into my brain
            The simple knowing that I was then within a sacred domain
            A pure space reserved for beauty and beauty alone
            A beauty that knows everything as its very own

So I alerted my vision and looked around with hope
To see how beauty might invite me into its expansive scope
It was then that it happened so quickly yet sweetly
That Beauty herself appeared she greeted and spoke to me
Come travel with me said Beauty with love and inspiration
I will show you my creation my elegant manifestation
And reveal to you how I fill every space and inspire every imagination

      I was amazed and entranced as you can plainly see
      For Beauty had never before simply appeared to me
      So I followed her lead with excitement and speed
    As Beauty lead me to the womb of our welcoming earth
    The planet where you and I dwell often ignoring its worth
      So the tour did begin and what a tour it was
  It changed me forever surely it was an initiation from above
Beauty showed me the seas the mountains the earth's forms galore
    Teeming with a majesty that I could but only adore

She opened my view to her budding plants her treasured trees
They captured my heart and filled me with such glee
Then I saw animals and fish and anything I could wish
and nature's lively air her pure elegance her utter flair

Beauty stopped for a moment and whispered in my ear
That the best was next a creation I would surely find dear
Yes she showed me human beings like I'd never viewed them before
I spied their splendor beheld their beauty and glimpsed their grace
As the utter wonder of this creation named human race
Awoke excited elation in every pore of my face

I saw at once the divine charm of this form
Its brilliance its glory in such majesty adorned
        To be human and aware to be human and know
        Are joys and treasures that emit a special glow
                To be human and love to be human and feel
                Hold a blessing and power that still make me reel

I returned to my swing that sways above this sphere
Where infinity glows and eternity flows everywhere
And I looked at earth anew through gratefully transformed eyes
I now see beauty's home where her unbridled grandeur lies
Where the domain and realm of beauty's grace
Has claimed us as her most beauteous space
Has created us as her human race

Delight

It happened one day as I attended to my oughts
Engaged and lost in my very important thoughts

That I noticed a strange but quite charming sight
I saw a man actually experiencing delight
Yes finding delight in everything in his sight

I saw him laugh openly as he watched children play
He felt the fruits relished the scents of the market's vast display
He tasted the sweetness that the smallest touch could bestow
While looking at it all with eyes fully aglow

He's truly present I thought he doesn't just survive

He's fully engaged really here not just half alive

He's focused and attentive to whatever comes his way

So very present to life's every unexpected play

How impressive he was this man of simplicity
This humble representative of life's hidden felicity
I confess that in my own complexity my very bright stupidity
I had simply forgotten had failed to see
The delicious delicacy of each day's simple activity

As I savored his delight at all these coincidences
I came suddenly to my own senses I lost my careful defenses
I realized the truth that this ordinary sage so artfully displays
That fascination can be found in every day's mystery-filled maze

On that day I awoke I opened to the delight
Inherent in everything in my previously dulled sight
The singing birds the quiet breeze the soft smells of spring
The wonders that are veiled or are often unforeseen
Yes I opened my eyes to whatever might cross my path
And to its gifts that invite my senses to a now delight-filled bath

Now I look at the open sky or see the leafy trees
Look into your sweet eyes or feel the unseen breeze
Drink in the sun's rays or peer through the day's haze
I find the wonder the marvel the hidden surprise
Of the lows the highs or the cloudy sunrise

Delight oh delight you've captured my sight
Whatever I notice I call now to my focus whether vital or trite
The smallest detail the tiniest of life's twists
I behold its beauty as it invites me to a bliss
That seemed earlier unachievable but is now quite believable

Delight oh delight I've found your veiled treasure
In this world's display of sensual pleasure
Chaos or perfection or whatever lies between
Now ignites my heart with its delicious theme
As it sparks my life and gives me the steam
That allows each day to fulfill my most hidden dream

Delight oh delight I await you tonight

What's It All About

What's it all about
Why are we here what does it mean
This purpose of life this human scene
Who are we anyway why do we even care
It's hard trying to be so humanly aware
Figuring it out can just make us scream

We give it our best shot the old college try
Examining the facts then wondering why
We're baffled bemused befuddled and confused
So we think it through we even ask the Muse

Is it all by chance or are we here by design
Perhaps we're created perfect then again you don't look so sublime
Surely we're all evolving but maybe six days is all it takes
Existence really seems absurd but this destiny thing feels pretty great
Is it 'I think therefore I am' or maybe 'to be or not to be'
Is it all about us or perhaps only about me

Surely we'll get it right one of these years
The answer to this question that burns between our ears
Who am I why am I here
The question seems simple why does it trigger such fear
I'll think about it later for now where's the beer

Well it finally happened one day I was thinking so hard
My brain swelled so big after consulting the bard
That it exploded yes it did all over the walls
It blasted through the doors and burst down the halls
A messy scene it was it took days to clean up
But my mind was now gone the jig was up

    With nowhere else to go I collapsed into my heart
    Where that question of all questions simply fell apart
    My heart smiled at me sweetly with tender emotion
    Could it be about love it asked me with gentle devotion

Could it be about love I repeated my heart's question
Then listened within me as it circled round my digestion
So simple so easy so pure so clear
Even elegant and inviting nothing austere
Yes! I heard from the depths of my being
It is about love so let's flow with love's seeing

Since then I let go I surrendered to my heart
Where all questions instantly transform into love's art
Now I ask not what does it mean
I sit in my heart and watch love create the scene
I see beauty and wonder elegance and grace
Everywhere I turn they're quietly there in my face

    I love you I love you that's all I can now say
    And I'll love you always day after day

Eagle's Eye

Have you seen the space that thrives above the forest of our lives
How grand it is what breadth it gives what vision it spies
No wonder the birds that claim these skies seem so wondrously free
As they glide so gracefully above earth's open canopy

Oh to be a hawk a falcon an eagle a raven

And see life's grand schemes its far reaching themes it secreted haven

If bird we could be what might we now see or perhaps envision

That as ordinary mortals seems beyond our so limited vision

If you were a bird flying above this forest of life
What think you might your vast vision be like
As you soar sweep scan sway and circle in flight
As you fly free unfettered unbounded
The spaciousness that captures your view just might leave you astounded
And the awe that fills your endless sight render you dumbfounded

In a moment of surprise a strange question circled 'round my mind
Is there inside me the same vision perhaps my own eagle's eye
That offers me that ceaseless view afforded by the mile high sky
Is there concealed somewhere within me a knowing as vast as infinite space
An inner bird that soars freely sees clearly and can fill me with vision's grace

I listened with my inner ear as it probed the echoes of my core's deep sphere
To see if perhaps some bird could be heard or that inner vision stirred
"I'm here! I'm here?" I heard these surprising words from deep inside

It was my own inner bird my infinite soul that soars so wide
"As above so below!" The voice continued to impart
"Whatever flies boundlessly above and sees the forest's true art
Soars equally far-seeingly in the lower skies of your very own heart"

Yes I discovered there is an eagle within It's right here
With an eyesight so vast a vision so clear
A knowing that's pure and a wisdom without peer
It lives within the forest of my own soaring soul my own winged mind
And flies with the same freedom that the birds find so kind

Come join me in this inner eagle's nest now so near
And share with me this clear seeing sphere
Where the air is pure the vision is sure the sounds are clear
Where we know life's secrets so cleverly hidden within the forest's dimmer light
Where life swiftly appears bright and the view quickly becomes a delight
Where we can frolic play skip laugh and leap
And where we can finally the forest's gifts enjoy and its rewards reap

So bring on the birds that live within our hearts
Unleash the inner eagle that soars within and the wisdom it imparts
And unveil the view that our soul brings from on high
We are free you and I ... with wings so alive and spry
With wings that allow us to soar to fly to ascend to the sky

Feel the breeze enjoy the ease claim the space
Where spirit excites us where clarity delights
Where God gives us such endless grace

Forgiveness

I found my friend anguished and in pain
From being mocked and scorned yet again
Oh how it hurts he said how it weighs me down
To be insulted and wronged to be the target of frown

The pain it brings me the damage I feel
Ought to be duly avenged so I might heal
The wrongdoer should pay for his crime serve his time
Be punished and pained so my innocence can be re-gained
Surely I'll feel better I might even find pleasure
If the villain feels my strain and knows that pain that refuses to wane

I witnessed how my friend's poor luck left him feeling so bitterly stuck
Yet I felt his heart's affection wanting only to relieve him of his deep infection
I sensitively asked my friend does your heart still feel okay
Has your loving spirit somehow survived this terrible day

He looked silently at me knowing just what I meant
Then gave me a growing smile that his own feeling heart surely had sent
My heart seems just fine he replied exposing a look of relief
And I'm now ready to hear my heart's more far-sighted belief

His heart then opened wide and began its unique vision to confide
Life seems so cruel it said and so unfair but there's a bigger picture I'd like to share
May I now show you my special vision my more soul-filled rendition

We let such hurt into our lives his heart now advised
So that we can broaden our narrow boundaries and expand our lives
We allow ourselves to suffer not so others will be our enemy
But to allow our heart's love to nurture us and build our own identity

The villains we hate may also serve as angels that help create our fate
The perpetrators of our deepest pain also promote our personal gain
We allow their painful storm so that we can grow and magically transform
We experience their humiliation so that love can bring about our own magnification

So first take a fresh look at those who bring grief to your soul
And consider thanking them then for playing that villainous role
That now allows you to grow beyond your own self-dug hole
When you look afresh at what they send you might even see them as your friend

Forgive them then ... forgive them ... and forgive them anew
So that you can feel my love and my invitation to renew
Forgive and forgive until your hurt and anger no longer live
Until the pain of the event turns into a chorus of inner content

Forgive ... forgive and forgive without end
Until the whole world becomes a welcomed friend
Until your previous pain feels like a God-given gain
Until your love-packed heart is fully in charge
And your whole life becomes beautifully and delightfully large

Forgive and forgive then every day
And I your heart will escort you to love in every possible way

Imagine That

Have you ever seen a giant green gorilla
Playing pleasurably in a shiny shimmering sandbox
Or a rosy red rhinoceros
Shaping salty sandcastles on a beauty-blanketed beach
Or a wingless wondrous white horse
Flying freely flowingly through a splendidly spacious sky

If indeed you have
Well then you may just be on the verge
Of glimpsing an even more inspiring more stirring sight
Waiting just for you right in the middle of your endless imagination

It's a singularly splendid sight you understand
One never before seen even sensed by anyone anywhere
Perhaps it wasn't even possible to have been pictured or imagined
Because a wildly way out mind wacky and willing enough to witness it
Had never appeared on our puffy powdery planet until ...
Well until one strange day you walked onto our silly scene

So fix your mind's mighty eye upon an inspiring image now ready to emerge
Let your spirit lift you to heights your imagination move you to sights
That will fill your brain with unexpected lights and bring you delicious delights
Get ready for the most remarkable ride of your life

There it is you can see it now
A glistening gleaming light gently glowing in your silent soul
Its luminescence filling the empty endless spaces of your awareness
It calls to you to enter softly into its compelling caring chamber
Into a new wondrous world where plentiful priceless gifts permeate the void

You peer passionately into these grace-filled gratifying gifts
You watch their endless elegance expand before your excited eyes
Only to be instantly dazed dazzled bedazzled
By their stunning splendor their magical majesty

I've just stepped in to become a part of a wildly wondrous world
You say to yourself as you ingest digest this sacred satisfying sight
A realm of light a dimension of life that has invisibly inhabited my soaring spirit
From the magical mysterious moment of my human birth
But was silent and unseen by my supple sprightly senses until now

A world beyond where gorillas rhinoceroses and horses
All move in rhythmic response to life's mythical and magical forces
A world felt only beyond the senses known only outside my mind's fences
A world now tangible touchable true and real
Even if only to my soul's still knowing my spirit's silent zeal

It's here it's here this way out wordless wonder
Glowing in my core alive in every pore now audible in its quiet roar
Life's magical marvel its generous genius its now personalized power
It's here in my heart animated in my mind and alive in my life
Here for me to feel it to know it to embrace it even to become it
From now on every day for the rest of my life
Forevermore
Imagine that

Breath of Fresh Air

Ah the sumptuous savory splendor of air
How privileged we are to breathe this formless wonder
To inhale and exhale this invisible delicacy of life
To feel its nurturing gifts flowing through our body's waiting cells

What is this mysterious miracle of nourishment that we call air
This precious prana this enchanting chi this life force of nature
That we so endlessly bring into our hungry needful bodies
then so freely give back to the unknown source whence it came

What an amazing marvel this ethereal energy is
As it silently strokes us with the sensual embrace of space itself
And selflessly serves us the delectable drink of infinity's cosmic caring

> *To breathe this air is to know intimacy with life itself*
> *To feel God's endearing love flowing sweetly though our bodies*
> *To taste heavenly honey in our yearning beating hearts*
> *And to digest infinity's radiance in our now satisfied senses*

And on this playful planet where creativity has named and claimed the game
Could it be that with each intimate intake of life's bountiful breath
Our earth mother feeds us her fantasy-rich formula for magical living
And writes into our willing cells her personally patented prescription
For instantly awakening us to our planet's juicy aliveness
As she ever so gently wraps us in the loving embrace of her bountiful chi

What an honor to experience endless infinity making love to us
To feel life's beauty flowing intimately through our needful bodies
To have nature's healing touch so sweetly kiss our eager skin
Each time we breathe this gracious gift called air

When we take in life's precious prana its cherished chi
We are no longer alone no longer separate no longer a stranger
When we inhale this mystical blessing of infinity into our lungs
Our bodies instantly know the bountiful blessing of grace
That has just become a loving part of who we are

Is it possible that God's very being is strangely alive in this wordless marvel
That the divine's living light is gift wrapped in its tender touch
That infinity's never ending love is enveloped in its invisible embrace

What an ecstatic gift it is to be renewed by this priceless work of art called air
As we feel its tender transforming kiss moving across our suggestible skin
Its elegant caress magically energizing our body's most far reaching molecules
Its penetrating infusion of indulgent love blessing our every human need

Can you experience air's unexplainable bliss
Now tickling the soft sensitivities of your deepest emotion
Its shameless love nourishing your once heavy heart
Its generous grace flowing warmly through your body's compliant muscles
As with every breath your lungs cry out in celebration of life's endless senseless splendor

Thank you gentle air priceless prana charming chi
For delivering the endless gifts of God's creation so generously to me
through every inhale and exhale of my breath-filled life

There's a Field ...

Out beyond notions of right and wrong of good and bad
There's a sacred field where we meet all equally clad
It's an open field a caring space hosting endless grace

Out beyond ideas of pretty and ugly of fat and thin
There's a sacred field where we meet without our judgment's din
A field where affection and perfection are our only connection

Out beyond our cultures and races and separate traditions
There's a sacred field where we meet with no ambitions
It's a field of union of embrace of shared fruitions

Out beyond practices of pride and prejudice of war and peace
There's a sacred field where we sweetly meet and greet
A field where the purest love fills the space and creates the heat

Out beyond worlds of separation individuation and segregation
There's a sacred field where we meet without trepidation
A field of true humanity of blended family of shared sensation

Yes out beyond our cherished beliefs and treasured creeds
Our prized principles that tout such acceptable deeds
There's a sacred field where we meet and finally feel freed
A field where devotion and mutual promotion are the rules we heed

I love this field it feels like my only true home
It's a holy place where our real selves can roam
A pure space where shameless freedom is at large
A warm dwelling where our shared heart is now in charge

In this sacred field we behold the holy and divine
In this hallowed temple we find in ourselves what is truly sublime
In this quiet sanctuary we are touched by each other's beauty
And in this consecrated shrine we find that love is our only duty

In this precious residence we find anew our inborn innocence
In this field of peace where love once again makes seamless sense
Where we can play and embrace in a joy-filled space
And where soul shares the central place with life's amazing grace

Let's live in this field you and I every day
Roll in its sweet grass and learn anew how to play
Let's invite its simplicity to take over our mind
And let its wonder become our hearts' treasured find

In this sacred field of light of love of simple truth
We'll live life in the timelessness of never ending youth
In this field of beauty wonder and awe sublime
We will discover anew creation's original design

Yes in this sacred field of serenity of infinity of endless grace
You and I will meet face to face in a daily embrace
As we enjoy the gifts of a better than ever human race

Reflections

Reflections

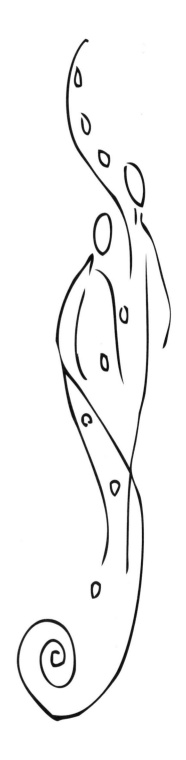

Also by Bill Bauman

OZ POWER! How to Click Your Heels and Take Total Charge of Your Life

- Paperback book
- Audio book, read by author
- Companion: Inspirational Thoughts for Your Life's Journey
- Video DVD and audio CD format: Presentation by Bill Bauman

SOUL TALK The soul's four gifts: truth, power, love and empowerment

- DVD or audio CD format

LIVING WITH GRACE Its loving qualities and its invitation to blessings

- DVD or audio CD format

FINDING YOUR INNER TRUTH Discover your innate love, wisdom and truth

- DVD or audio CD format

LIFE'S THREE ESSENTIAL TOOLS Invitation to power, love, and consciousness

- DVD or audio CD format

INNER JOURNEYS ... OUTER MASTERY

- Four volumes, each containing four audio CDs:
  - Volume I: *The Real You ... Finding Purpose in Life ...*
    How Vast is Your Vision ... Living in the Moment
  - Volume II: *The Spirit of Forgiveness ... Welcoming Life's Gifts ...*
    The Many-Faceted You ... Living with the Coyote
  - Volume III: *Finding Your Inner Beauty ... Me, a Mystic? ...*
    Life!—the Soul's View ... A View from Above the Forest

SOUL VISION A modern mystic looks at life through the eyes of the soul

- Paperback book

Find full product descriptions and direct purchase information:
Center for Soulful Living
www.aboutcsl.com